I'M IN LOVE
WITH TWO GIRLS

Richard James Allen

ALSO BY RICHARD JAMES ALLEN

The World's Gone Mad…Hasn't It? (2010)

I'M IN LOVE
WITH TWO GIRLS

POEMS FROM THE DOWNLANDS
TO THE SEA

Richard James Allen

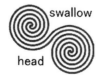

Swallowhead Publishing 2010

SWALLOWHEAD PUBLISHING
3 The Green, Calne, Wiltshire, SN11 8DG
www.swallowhead.co.uk
info@swallowhead.co.uk

British Library Cataloguing in Publication Data.
A catalogue record for this book is available
from the British Library

ISBN: 978-0-9564844-1-3

Design and Typeset by
Jim and Peggy Grich at *eBookProducers*
All Photography by the Author

Printed and bound by Lightning Source UK Ltd, Chapter House, Pitfield, Kiln Farm, Milton Keynes, MK11 3LW

ONCE AGAIN THIS BOOK IS DEDICATED TO MUM, DAD,
PETE, MICHELLE AND ALDA.

I ALSO GRATEFULLY ACKNOWLEDGE THE INSPIRATION OF
THE MANY WRITERS AND POETS I HAVE BEEN
LUCKY ENOUGH TO ENCOUNTER, INCLUDING:
THE WRITERS OF THE I CHING, BJÖRK, IVOR CUTLER,
RAM DASS, SIDSEL ENDRESSEN, MARIA LAURETTE
FRIIS, LAOZI (LAO TSE), SHANE MCGOWAN, AND
WILLIAM SHAKESPEARE.

CONTENTS

Preface

Welcome. This is the second of a pair of books, which together form a collection of my poetical works to date. This is the Yin/Heaven book to balance the Yang/Hell of its fiery companion; *"The World's Gone Mad...Hasn't It?"* In the preface of that book, I recount the moment on Lake Titicaca when the poet in me was awakened. The poem "On Lake Titicaca", which appears in this volume, is a fragment of that epiphany. Although most of the poems here were written after 2002, there are a handful of poems like "On Lake Titicaca" that go back as far as 1990, for example, "Desert Sea" and "Another Pulse of Unreason."

In contrast to the disturbing, angry, sometimes ranting tone of the first book, these poems deal primarily with the subjects of love, loss and landscape. Wherever I have lived, I have always measured the landscape with my body through the act of walking. Wiltshire's open downland around Avebury and near my home in Calne has been a huge influence on my writing. Sometimes I take a camera or sketchpad with me, but I derive most satisfaction from having my strongest experiences resurface later as poetry. As well as this relationship with the landscape, turbulence in my personal relationships has also acted as a major catalyst for many of the poems in both books.

I have noticed that my sensitivity to my emotional body varies greatly. At the times when I feel most closely in touch with a particular emotion I immediately try to record the experience with words, aiming to make the most direct transference from heart to paper. My writing methodology also embraces writing when I don't feel like writing, recording dreams immediately upon waking, and writing either side of sleep when I am in a relaxed, day-dreamy, slightly detached mood.

My poetry does not consciously concern itself with traditional forms, although elements of those forms can be found. For example, some poems could be described as lyrical or elegiac. In general I am drawn more to poets outside of the discredited and moribund western canon. My influences are more pop-culture than high-culture and more rapper than rondeau. It seems to me that everywhere there are hip-hoppers, def-jammers and skilled slammers, so I hope you enjoy my flavour of versification.

Once again my thanks go out to everyone who has helped with the production of this book: Alda, Mum and Dad, Francesca Bell, Jude Allen and Angela King. Special thanks are due to Peggy and Jim Grich at eBookProducers. Lastly I would like to thank everyone who has ever encouraged or supported me in any way, including those who have bought a copy of one of my books.

Richard

Summer Solstice 2010

Spike you were right

We'd be daft not to laugh!

Part I

Landscape

Land is just sea in slow motion

Welcome Back

Welcome back to Wessex
This land of white horse vales
I hope the gentle breath of real good fortune
Touched you on your trails

So once again at this week's end
We will walk upon her warm sweet form
Touch toes on loam
Cross spring's magic foam
And make our way
To where stone giants lay
Where time stands still
Or maybe runs away

Richard Allen

Waterfall

Shimmering sparkle life
Rainbows in every pregnant drop
Waterfall
Energising my spirit
Bringing easy gentle flow

Equal in sun or shade
Unfolding in drought or rain
Leaving behind calming
Soothing stillness
To heal our lives

At West Kennet Long Barrow

The gateway to our ancestors was patrolled by
two gliding shadow sentinels
We have come so near now that they materialize
Youthful
Fast
Graceful
As innocent as the universe

Richard Allen

Pen y Beacon (Hay Bluff)

Human sounds move easily to my pricking ears
Running
Whinnying
Brown and white blotch-patterned ponies
Free as wind
Fuss warning

Scattered psilocybic sheep
Spring water gurgles cleanly underground
Beneath rocks and moss
And lichen frozen dwarfs
To feed the raw flesh mushroom
That bluffs back a threat to the mammal
presence

At Wayland's Smithy

Smiles and sun and birds rejoice
But ritual has gone from here to other galaxies
for vibrant death
Sail on the breeze across other nights
To return here one day
And find true voice

Richard Allen

Christmas Walk

Hissing hedge
You put me on edge
What might I have done?
Back in a month when spiders could fly
And ants could ask why?
This is the day I'll look for clear sky
Not dwell on a time when poppy buds burst
Or eating worm castes gave me a thirst
For fruit from the tree that might help me to see

Rustling grass
You have shown me the path
To the top of the hill
Creatures of night
You've shown me the light
How to have all my thrills
To drink 'til I'm filled
Yet keep me from ills

Goose bumps
Cows graze humps
Shadows and lines
It's nearly the time to finish this rhyme
And descend in my prime

Stone Thunderbolt

Out on the windy downs
Stands a silver circle of stones
It's been there longer than anyone can
remember
And it will be there when we're dead and gone

More than just for tourists
It's there to guide us
We navigate the universe
It makes the invisible visible when we are
blinded

Out on the rainy downs
We soak our souls in shared history
Connecting
Plugging in
Transmitting and receiving eternity

The stones are our compass
We turn towards our God
We stand in the clear light
And touch the source

Out on the chalky downs
A winged horse takes us to the underworld
On the sun-bleached downland grass
We roll and laugh

Stone thunderbolt

Richard Allen

"Crop Circle"
monochrome collagraphic print by the author

Look from Your Window

Look from your window
Raise your senses to the heavens
The sons and daughters of the sun are gathered
to ring great changes

Jupiter
Riding from the south
Has invited us to join him high on a white
stallion for two moons

Mars
Satisfied with his violent influence of recent
times
Now moves calmly away from the ram to look
for a bull

Virgo's emissary
Spica
Smiles proudly and foolishly at the earth sign's
close sibling Venus

Look from your window!

Richard Allen

March

Earrings of dew on a tomato seedling
Hyacinth perfume playing on the breeze
Blossoms like coconut ice sweeten my world view
It is that time of year again
The lowering sun warms my face and neck
Light and carefree robin song is alive with the
hope and optimism attendant at the birth of this
new season

Dog Rose

Dog Rose
How did you get your name?
You're no dog
Not pug
Nor ugly
You're never an imposition
Or ill-mannered
You're not a dog at all!

Cerise delight
You're a passionate
Overflowing
Summer charm
A wild rose

Richard Allen

England

My England keeps growing
Birdsong in the morning
Cool fog on sea swirling
Soft green warmth
Spring turning
Up with the lark
Up with the lark and we're flying

Brothers and Cousins
Conkers and paddling
Cold hands and feet
Cold sea
Wet leaves
Stone walls straddling

England it's you
England it's you
It's me

April sun
Warm my neck
June wind
Hail sting my face
Stand by beech
Stand by oak
Stand by ash and birch
And yew
Yes you
Only you will know

I've been to the Indies
I've been round the world
Near and far
Pretty and plain
But there's only one place I'd choose to remain

You are my England
Your rivers are my blood
You are my every breath
My passion's in flood
You are my Avon
My Trent and my Thames
You are my ship
My sails
My friend

Richard Allen

Untitled photograph by the author

Butterflies and Elephants

Butterflies and elephants
Chimpanzees and parakeets
Big blue sea and fluffy clouds
Dreaming in our wonderland

She's my love
Oh she's my love

Baby moles and bright red ants
Jellyfish and stripy pants
Floating in a sea of love
Looking at the sky above

Big world of ours you're beautiful
Big world of ours you're wonderful

Hot air balloons and oak tree roots
Swinging bats and tall top hats
Gran and Pops and boys and girls
All living in our special world

Oh life of ours you're beautiful
Oh life of ours you're wonderful

Richard Allen

Marezige at Night

Everyone is sleeping in Marezige
Everyone is dreaming down our little lane
Except for the nightingale
Except for the moon
Except for the mouse who knows the cat is
coming soon

Everyone is sleeping in Marezige
Everyone is dreaming down our little lane
Little children's dreams float above the roofs
Swirling through the valley to the spirit world

Everyone is sleeping in Marezige
Everyone is dreaming down our little lane
Animals and adults healing all their wounds

Calm and stillness coming
From moon to earth to moon

Sleeping
Sleeping
Dreaming
Dreaming

Istria

Diamond sentinels flirt with the shore
People lost in thought
Terns weave
Rippled green blue light
Dark beast or mirror universe
Timeless tides of tranquility and war
Giving or taking
Men and women as rock hewn by wind and water
Lives shaped by tumbling seasons
Sorrow and Joy
Iron hues
Purple vines
Istria

Richard Allen

On Lake Titicaca

It's that magical place again
Fantasy land
Just like the glittering expansive salt lake

The water's so calm and gentle
The sky so clear and blue
Innocent painted clouds hang on every horizon
Slipping into the invisibility of other worlds
Through the thin air veil of distance

These gringos are friends now
Just like the mountains (some living with
clouds)

Hypnotic place
You are all the memories that probably never
were
All the mirages
Yet you are real
And I've been tricked into thinking that colours
weren't colours at all
But simply a dream
An Island
A dream

Desert Sea

I feel as though I'm in a dream
A romantic soft focus novel
It is set in a time gone by
Perhaps several hundred years ago

The future congeals
And I am stationary for maybe two minutes
I am not alone
I am in paradise

A wave a mile long is crashing in the desert
A scattering of rocks the size of skyscrapers is
rising from the haze
Ancient guardians of a personal dream

Richard Allen

Part II

Love

I would go off the edge of our flat world with you
Walk over land to Marrakech or Katmandu

You Are

You are the gentle sun
That warms my glinting granite shoulders
You are the soft wind
That whispers in my verdant leaves
You are the beautiful snow
That swaddles my soil with the warmth of
imagination and future
You are the generous bounty
That feeds my hungry woodland beast
You are the firm rain
That moistens my earthy mushroom seed
Because me
I'm you
And you
You're me

Richard Allen

On the Wings of My Mind

On the wings of my mind
I soar to your light
To be by your side
For night after night

Watching you drift
On the tides of your dreams
Hoping I'm with you
Giving life meaning

Chant Your Life

Chant your life
As the night's silver streamers light our hearts
On this transparent spring veil
Clear as a bell
Healing existence
The universe calls

At The House

Sadness and loss descended on my empty heart
when I first went to the house
Our two ghosts were living there
Laughing and playing

On a rainbow rug
A sunburnt nose
Warm wind tickling happy toes
Dreaming under swelling fruit
Among the nettles and insects
In a corner of the greenest garden
By a mossy bench propped up on crumbling
bricks

Amidst the swaying grasses
Spiders
Beetles crawling
Wild flowers wild smelling
As happy and carefree as summer itself

Eating cherries
Juicy games
Tomorrow never comes
The energy of a magic rising
Until all we can do is cry with joy
And hold each other tightly

Please look me in the eyes once more
Swim with me there
For I know you've been as seasick as me in this
ocean of hurt and uncertainty

Trust I no longer have a foot in two boats
I am steering a steady course
Aboard our coracle of love and truth

We're heading for the underworld
The Earth
The Mother
Our fingers and language and hearts entwined

Richard Allen

Two Stars

For you I'd walk all day and through the night
I'd make the journey without a light
Because you're my guide
You're so alive
You lift me up and make things right

I'm so impatient for the key
To take us out
To be free
So what's the answer in this world
For two stars floating in the universe?

Sweet Angel

I'd seen her at a fair up on the hill
I'd seen her in a peaceful dell
I went to her one night for her sweet sweet song
And there I travelled through a veil

Into her beauty's spell
I couldn't speak
And knew not where I was
Transfixed
Transformed
In paradise
My skin both cool and warm

Who is this girl
This rose
This fairy child?
Who is this sweet angel fluttering in my mind?
I cannot say even to this day
Yet hope and pray "True Love" I'll say
Before life runs away and it's all too late

Richard Allen

Something We Both Share

When we met the ground was wet
But my heart was warm
As we chased fauns

We climbed a hill
And with a thrill
Were swallowed by the earth and sky

Lying down in summer grass
I dreamed with you
Of how we'd live and laugh

Clouds gathered for us both
Despite feeling close
Were shipwrecked in a storm

Reborn

The ocean's scent was heaven sent
Stones warmed by sunshine
Sublime

Love
Lovers
Dream
Dreamers

Now parted once again
A never ending chain it seems
Do we still share a dream?

Untitled photograph by the author

Come To Me

You are as vital to me as the air I breathe
Without you I suffocate and die

How can I not be with you?
It just doesn't feel right
Why do I continue to act the fool
While casting you in the stooge's role?

I feel empty without your beauty and danger
next to me.
Achievements seem futile without your support
of reinforced concrete

Please come to me
Bring your treasures
Your magic
Your clarity

I will grow to be a man one day soon
So your children will have a genuine father
Not a clown
A jester or goon

Please come to me
Merge your open sky with my tight earth
So we are a landscape of the universe
Boundless and timeless
Riding death and birth

I Feel Her

When hailstones fall
I feel her
When gentle winds call
I feel her
When heaven kisses earth
I feel her
We're not together now
But I feel her
Once upon a time we danced through the
garden
I still feel her
I am waiting for her song
I don't care how long
In the end we'll both come home
I will feel her

Richard Allen

At Callanish (Golden Eagle Wings)

Over pale moors
I love her
Through the dark black lochs
I love her

Oh how we laughed and ran across the sky
Oh how we played
How we tumbled
How we cried

Over peat cut land
I love her
Through the standing stones
I love her

Oh how we held each other close so very tight
To keep out the cold of the northern summer
nights

Golden eagle wings
She loves me
Swoop and catch our love
She loves me

Oh how we shared all the beauty of this land
Timeless and dreamless
Perfection in our hands

At Oldbury Hill Fort
(Earth Sign Essence)

I want to smell your sickly sweet perfumed
rotting leaves
I want to smell your body odour
Fungus must musk
I want to put fresh young grass in my mouth
For its dewy seasoning to make me feel closer
to you

Quench my thirst
I want snowflakes on my hot tongue
Hard ice pushed against my vulnerable naked
heat
Caress me with your petrifying strength
Freeze my ears with your frosty winter breath
Frighten me with your shrill dry leaf call in fall

I want to take a handful of your summer
sunshine butter
And smooth it over my shoulders
My buttocks and my breast

I must feel soft mud squeeze between my
fingers
Squelch between my toes
I have got to be immersed in loam
To drown in you
Become the earth
So once again spring's rain can wash me clean

Richard Allen

Words Are My Tools

Words are my tools
They turn my dreams
They ratchet love
The world to heal

Swallows' sky to blue moon's night
Life's warm laugh to freedom's light

Lay down your specs
Lay down your pen
Lay down your maps
Lay down your gin
Lay down your clothes
And stop your roads

Look to the sky
Look to the leaves
Look to the earth
Look to the breeze

A loving home from which to roam
Look for the doves
The return of love

You Know

That night we passed
The night we laughed
By the way I love you

I want to touch your toes
I want to touch your clothes
I want to kiss your eyelids
I want to kiss your nose

Toes so pink and straight
They smell of you
Your eyelids hide your world
It's so soft
So you

I might send you a card
Saying "Love isn't fair"
I don't think you know who I am
But deep down inside you know I was there

Richard Allen

Thank You

Thank you for your open door
Your cup of hope
Bowl of wisdom
Your stories long
Thanks for walking
Laughter and a little Qigong

Oh magical equinox energy
Spring's dove of peace has descended to touch us
Make us shine
Make us sparkle like the stars
Make us cry tears of pure joy
As the gentle dawn whispers its signal for change

The Sarsen Trail

Dance a happy Neolithic way
While angels sing for the moons of May
Wings from your slender ankles sprout
Fountains of achievement spout

May you be carried high and smiling on the
back of the little bear for the last six miles

Richard Allen

A Love Poem

I miss you on the sunny days
I miss you on my joyful days
I need you on the cloudy days
I need you on my stormy days

I want to hold you tight
I want to be with you every night
Nothing can touch me when you're there for me
Pain slips away
Horrors fade from me

Let's not let life rush past without us really
loving
Everyone in separate bubbles
Everyone with separate troubles
Everyone in separate heads
In separate cars
In separate lives
In separate beds

Let's glide in the gentle stream of life together
Before we're washed out to sea
And battered among ruthless waves
Because that is how it will be unless we act now
Ourselves to save

Nature's Perfect Mates

A king without a queen
Stupidity and fate
Fairytales and tragedies
At the bottom of a lake

Magic touch without a cheek
Laughing smile
Oh playful thing
Now buried by the weeks

Head heart and stomach empty
Observation's blank
Imprisoned by the freedom
To rob emotion's bank

So join me on a handsome horse
And we'll ride the moonlit forests
Of imagination's verse
Yes we'll ride the moonlit landscape

As nature's perfect mates

Richard Allen

I Want

I'm sitting in a lonely room with tear-stained eyes
A helpless fool
Please tell me why

You say you don't know my intentions
You say that all now past was only a nice dream
A pleasant fantasy
But isn't it clear?
It is to me
You and I were meant to be

I want the moon to move us like plants
I want the wind to brush through our fur and
fingers
I want the rain to stick us together
I want to share our smell
I want the sun to anneal our will

I want to sway gently in the ocean's current with
you
I want to lose myself in your delicate sunlit hair
I want to breathe your salty corporeality into my
heart and lungs
I want to be carried away on the tides of your
touch
I want to be with you
Close again

Judas Kiss

Judas kiss fade to touch
Tears' crumbling and salty crust
Scar tissue sunset fade from view
Leave only now for me and you

In shelter by a river
Trees and sun made you peel off a layer
That's when I saw your shoulder blades
Oh! Soul did soar and loins did ache
Heart I swear you did miss a beat
And again later that day when I glimpsed your
feet
Girl what do you do to me?
For in my bed at night I cannot sleep

Richard Allen

To Cerne Abbas

We've walked upon the mother
On a star-crossed night
I hope it won't be long
Until we travel with the sun
To lie upon the father
And cultivate a union
On his giant's prick
So all our heart's desire
Has flesh and blood and bone

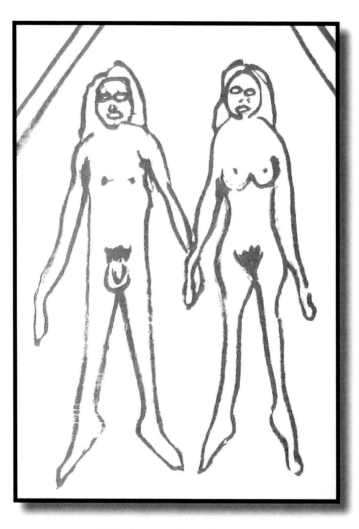

Untitled screen-print by the author

(original in colour)

Will You Stand By Me?

As I've tried to live my life these past few days
I've noticed most people seem to live their lives in
a haze

That's why I want a woman with clarity
I want a natural woman next to me
I want a loving woman by my side
It's not any woman I want
It's you I need in my life

Your gifts to me have made me the happiest man
alive
Nothing can compare to what we've shared
So it breaks my heart to be pushed away
For logic or self protection
Or fear of being betrayed

Yes I've got my faults
Haven't we all?
But I can't turn my love on and off
Like the lights in the bedroom or hall
So "yes" is the answer
I'll stand by your side
With all my strengths and all my weaknesses
Will you stand by mine?

Part III

Loss

*Use your heart to listen to both the audible, and
more importantly the inaudible
Know what you know, and more importantly know
what you don't know
Love both what is familiar, and more importantly
what is not familiar*

I Miss You

I missed you when I awoke alone
I missed you when I spoke alone
I missed you when I worked alone
I missed you when I rested on my own

I miss you when the sun is setting
I miss you when the moon is rising
I miss you when the stars are shining
I miss you when the owl is calling
I miss you when night's cold cloak is falling

I will miss you telling me I'm golden
I will miss seeing my other half unfolding
I will miss your every word and movement
I will miss your every in and out breath
I will miss you every second
Every heartbeat
Until death

Richard Allen

She's Gone

I met her through a dating agency
I'd been out with lots of other girls
But now I left no room for complacency
I thought this relationship must unfurl

Me to hers
Her to mine
Bit by bit I was led to dreamland
Both she and I were sat on cloud nine

I felt compelled to be with her
As she must be to be with me
Our love just grew and grew
It had no boundaries
It just felt really free

We started slowly
And there was really nothing wrong
But now she's gone
Oh now she's gone

Man and wife
And there was really nothing wrong
But now she's gone
Oh now she's gone

We just slipped apart
There's nothing wrong
We're free to roam
But now I find that I'm alone

Still Life Study (The Wall)

Framed by bed and ceiling
Light switched
Smudged and marked
A sensible friend for a wayward dangling
television cable

It is one in a million
Yet one of millions
Loyal and dignified
Yet cheap and ignored

This wall has flecks of chipped paint
And prisoners of foam fragments in its
magnolia matrix
It is beautiful

Married to the shadows of the contents of the
room
A dictionary
A clock
A pillow or human head
An ensemble that cast their nuances of light and
form
Leaving only stillness
Leaving only the wall

Richard Allen

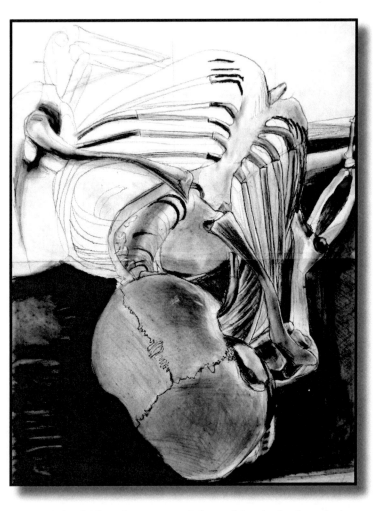

Untitled still-life study; compressed charcoal drawing by the author

Tears Just Seem to Fall

So much time has gone
Yet tears still seem to fall
When I think of you
My tears just seem to fall

At first it was all the time
Big red eyes of mine
I thought it would never end
A world without a friend

Wailing from my soul
I've dug myself a hole
This lonely single bed
Sobbing pillow wishing death

I hear your favourite song
I smell your favourite flower
Though it's been so long
I still count the hours

I dropped a gift you gave
And as I watched it break
My tears just seemed to fall
Tears just seemed to fall

Richard Allen

I hold your photograph
I can almost hear you laugh
Two halves taped as one
But my suffering goes on

I drive past our old life
Where we lived as man and wife
Regret's a deafening call
And tears just seem to fall

When I'm on my own
Lost and all alone
I sit and think of you
And tears just seem to fall

Lost

This is what I wanted so why am I so sad?
I've closed the door
Tears will fall
I'm going to feel real bad

Can self-esteem go from low to less?
Is it all my fault
This crazy mess?

Have I played a game with people's hearts?
If so
Right from the start I first fooled myself
I'm caught in my own web

I dream
Project
And make it all alright
But deep down inside I know we're leaving each
other's lives

So we won't get to the Eiffel Tower
We won't get to Central Park
Never again will we run through fields of wheat for
a lark
No huddling together in the crook of a tree
In the middle of the woods
Together but free

Leave Your Smell

Leave your smell
Leave your presence
I'll suck your absence in like perfume
Let me embrace your shadow
Your still warm footprints

I'd cross the night to see the place touched by
your light
Allow me to stand in my tears
In the cold shadows
In my fears
Let me watch you sleep
Warm me with your radiance

Where are you tonight oblivious of my passion?
Laughing no doubt
Alive and reckless
Bounties spilling from your table to feed
ungrateful greedy dogs

I'm in Love with Two Girls
(Come on Mate, Get on with It!)

I've got a block
I'm frozen
I can't function
I can't move on until I've sorted this mess
Made my decision

I'm in love with two girls
In love with two places
Two worlds

The upper part of my chest flutters
I gasp at the lightness
The nausea
As I glimpse a future in tatters

Confusion
An absentee
Illusion
A cage
A freedom
Guilt for me to carry
What if once we'd married?

Sifting through the issues
Trying to find bone not just tissue
Because it will all slip through my hands if I
dither and dather

A wishy washy guy
A fence sitter
A quitter
Running away from having a mission

So why don't you listen?
Get on with it mate!

For Michelle

You said I had never written you a poem
Only God knows why not
So here I go
Here's my shot

Sadness
Depression
Grief and all
I should have plenty of material

I love you today more than I ever have
So I can't understand the path I'm taking
For months now I feel that my mind has been
breaking

I would go to the ends of the earth for you
I would give everything for you
Yes
I would even lay my life down for you

So why oh why oh why
Did I have to make us both cry?
And why can't I get...

What's next?

Richard Allen

When the Sun Shines

I'm so sad when the sun shines
Because I could be with you
We could cool our bodies in the morning orchard
dew

I'm so sad when the sun shines
Because I should be with you
Gathering wild mushrooms
Picking autumn fruits

I'm so sad when the sun shines
Beauty's not there without you
Life's sweetness and passion are awakened with
you

I'm so sad when the sun shines
I have only eyes for you
I need your vision to light my life's road

I'm so sad when the sun shines
I'm so sad when the rainbow sparkles
I'm so sad when the fairies dance
I'm so melancholy in nature's trance

When we die we join the infinite
We will join Romeo and Juliet
Together again in paradise
Lovers again
Bodies entwined

Oh you mean so much to me
Oh you mean so very much to me

Richard Allen

Untitled marker pen drawing by the author

Are We Never?

Are we never again to hear sweet birdsong tease
us from our slumbers
Are we never again to chant a peaceful solstice
sunrise
Are we never again to circle Technicolor
megaliths or tender young beech trees
Are we never again to break friendship's bread
among our blessed friends
Are we never again to hear the distant roar of
lions on a still English evening
Are we never again to baptise our physicality in
the depths of hidden lakes
Are we never to travel to the silent eternity that
is the centre of the forest
Are we never to gaze across an emerald mirror
to an undiscovered continent
Are we never to dream in a heather moor's mist
Or run naked through a maze of pink sand
dunes
Are we never to touch an exotic city's secrets
with our lust for vibrant life
Are we never to float with summer's cobwebs
on the perfume of an ancient crop
Are we never to measure our new land with our
meditating bodies
Are we never to laugh together while watching
cosmic mice eat a blue cheese moon
Or a giant beetle roll the midnight sun

Richard Allen

Are our hearts so proud and foolish that we'll
deny our mortal failings
Are we never to weep with happiness as our
lives go round the universe again

I am Alone Without Her

I am utterly alone without her
Only she can touch me so deeply in that place
where comfort and connection dwell

My now stale friendships are without any
common ground
My family live in fantasy
In my trance of loss other human beings hardly
register in my field of awareness

All food tastes bland without her in my life
Wine has no purpose
Birdsong brings no joy
Discomfort has no benchmark

Richard Allen

Healing

When we lose we cry
But our tears will always dry

Then our love grows deeper
Our love grows softer
Our love just grows stronger

When we lose we are as vulnerable as a new
born baby
So we care for ourselves until we're ready to
start again

Tears return
We learn
The big wheel turns

I Ain't Found It Yet

I knew a boy who went out to work to feel a little
free
But freedom soon knocked that boy down onto his
knees

There was a rebel who went out to work to keep
the system off his back
But he crawled into a bottle that went by the name
of Jack

I met a man who went out to work to build himself
a life
But he found it wasn't easy
Like walking on the blade of a knife

I was told of a guy who went out to work to boost
his self esteem
But his ambitious bully of a boss just crushed him
under her heel

I had a friend who ran away
He spent two years in bed
The day that he went back to work that work just
shot him down dead

Richard Allen

Whether eighteen or eighty
You're always at square one
Just button your lip and walk the line
Is there really anything to find?

Well if there is
If there is
I ain't found it yet…

But I'm still looking

Your Poem

This is your poem
It's not just ink on the page
This poem means business
This poem's a trade

You said I never wrote poems for you
And I know you think different
But it just isn't true
Each onion I fried
Each joke that I tried
It was only ever for you

What did you want?
Dead ink in a book?
Or love spinning wildly?
Real
In a laugh or a look?

My words jumped from the page
Eager to breathe
Live life fully
Hoping never to fade

So take this tragic relic
And hold it close to your breast
It contains my very essence
It contains my very best

Richard Allen

Light Me Up Again

One day not long ago my light went out
My head went down
I started love's drought
My tears just flowed
I didn't know whether to come or go

The music stopped
The music just stopped
I couldn't even move
I couldn't think
I couldn't find a balm that soothed

Halfway between this world and the next
Going through the motions
But no not those
No emotions
No sex

Blank empty cardboard land
Personality hollowed out
Bland
Passion stolen by the sorrow man
Oh my darling won't you take my hand?

The last post has sounded
I am walking wounded
Heal my heart
Heal my soul
Don't leave me alone

Light me up again
Help me come alive
Light me up again
Help me to survive
Light me up again

Richard Allen

Part IV

Hope

Everything is Answers

Today is the Greatest Day of Your Life

Today is the greatest day of your life
Not yesterday
Not tomorrow

If you're cold and wet
Hungry or tired
Just try to recognize that today is the greatest
day of your life

If you're warm and cozy
And just been fed
Try not to forget that today is the greatest day of
your life

If you're suffering or in pain
If you're helpless
In a life shackled with chains
Let your spirit rise because you've realized

Today is the greatest day of your life
Not yesterday
Not tomorrow

Richard Allen

If your health just left town
And your body's shutting down
If your cash just went pop
Or your wife's been shot

Remember today is the one
Because it's all you've got

Everyone's an Island

Everyone's an Island so the saying goes
But I want to be part of an archipelago
To watch ships sail to and fro

The waters have been busy
Although clouds have gathered now
To send many vessels to hidden coves
Or down to dodge shoals

But clear skies will come again
Seeds will line my shore
The future holds a dappled shade
Under which many rippled waves
Will warmly kiss my sandy pores

Richard Allen

Untitled acrylic painting by the author (original in colour)

Song of Hope, Song of Peace

It's in your voice
Your calm warm tone
It's in your eyes of sparkling coals
It's in your gait of catlike grace
Your song of hope
Your song of peace

Please listen to your songs of hope
Listen to them around the globe
Please listen to your songs of peace
In the UK
USA
And Middle East

Richard Allen

Epiphany
(In the Telemarketing Room)

At this moment peace comes down
It fills me up with warmth and light
Time disappears and my soul takes flight

I look around at some young faces
And wonder do they feel it too
A perfect bliss to never lose

I hope my smile conveys this love
So we can share a perfect world
It probably doesn't
But I have hope
At any moment they can join the fold

Whoever or whatever God is seems really close
We just need to crack the code
Perfection is here all the time
It's constant
It is
It's ours
It's mine

In Love, In Peace, In Harmony

An ocean away
Torn in half
Over the hills
I hear her laugh
An invisible mend
A happy end
Seemingly without a care
In truth she hardly dares
Sadness can perhaps be kept at bay
By collecting small joys in a jar each day
So guide me world
Where is my truth?
I need your help to set me loose

Stuck inland
Or by the sea
Aboard a train
A car
Or plane

Free me from my sticky stuck
Unblock my mind of yicky yuk
Give me courage to break free
Live in this world
In love
In peace
In harmony

Richard Allen

Bolivian Space Dance

Where on earth do I belong?
I belong everywhere in the universe
I can see everything
I'm shooting through all and nothing
I am travelling a trillion times faster than the
future

I can narrow my horizon
And run with the wind
Float on this earth
And cut all my strings

Will you dance naked with me in the warm glow
of existence?

Another Pulse of Unreason
(Brain Racing)

Slithering off the edge of the reality sphere
Melting into the galaxy of the Rainbowdrome
where you can't quite touch anything
All is as distant as an image seen though
someone else's strong spectacles
Unfocused

This is a time of confusion
But conviction and sharpness will come

Richard Allen

Mellow 37

Thirty seven and I've hit the pause button
My life's flashing red alert
But I'm jumping for nothing
My ship has sailed
I've missed the boat
But I don't give a monkey's now I've learned to
float

I suspect it's my body
Like a wind-up clock
Only so many ticks
So many tocks
I saw a documentary that said it doesn't matter
Whether it's whales or frogs
They only have so many heartbeats before they
pop their clogs

Taking my time
Drawing each breath
Stopping for tea
Taking a rest
I think I know what I'm doing
But then maybe not
But with no road a wrong one
I'll join my own dots

No more decisions to make
I'm no more real
No more fake
Just letting stuff happen
Just trying to create
A world that counts to ten
Before it acts
Before it's then

The Great Escape

Every day we pay and pay
So we can live a normal way
Sliced bread and milk
A TV quiz so we can think
But not so much we try to link
Not so much we start to rise
And take it back from men who lie
Who wear suits and macs and bowler hats
With stacks of cash and Chelsea flats

I'm looking for a quick way out
I'm looking for the easy life
I'm looking for my slice of pie
I'm looking for my chance to shine
I'm looking for the great escape
I'm looking for an artful dodge
I'm looking for my gravy train
So I can be and burn a brighter flame

Working Man

Roy
Bob
Bill and Brian
In overalls are England's lions
Clocking on for another shift
Committed to their families
Committed to their factories

Dead
Dying
Or soon to be gone
Precision
Care
Love
Loyalty
Service life long

Peering over half moons
Micrometers and shims
Cup of tea and daily rag
Wife's packed lunch and ounce of shag
Pot of grease worn thin by use
Whitworth gauge and steel capped boots

Day after day you know your place
It might be safe
But you are a hero because you know life's not
a race

Carefully chosen history
Carefully chosen life
Small pleasures
Huge gains
Working man
Return like rain

Full

I wanted it to be different
I wished I'd made another choice
That was the moment
Why couldn't I find my voice?

So this is how it is
The damage has been done
There's no point regretting
It's the same for everyone

It's just called life
It's just called love
It happens every day
It's why we're here
It's why we're woman and man
We are the human race
And in the end it's why we ran

Once things have happened they've happened
Next move
Next go
I can't change anything now because it's gone

So I'm going to stand up tall
Extend to my full height
Stay true
Express myself
Believe in myself
Speak up
Grow up
Act up
Live up

And be full

It's all Different Now

Does anybody listen to an old rocker's words?
Can Pete Townsend still be heard?
Who says the windmill's stopped?
Or the deaf old geezer's life's a flop?

Brandy swapped for tea
There's sadness and dignity
The Who did it all
While we just went to the shopping mall

Fight back the tears
Because glory rains down for years
It's not being sentimental
It's just that life is beautiful

Again inspiration will come
Perhaps the greatest-ever song
So dust off your youthful senses
And once again we'll tear down fences

It's all different now anyway
Anyhow

Richard Allen

For Oli Goather

Reading Oli's rhyme
Hitting every pulse
Every beat
Right on time
Wrapped tight
For a young blood in a fight
For his life
For his pride
Sometimes enjoying the ride

Maybe seen 9 mile
Lifting white kids right up high
If you're a punk
Or a poet
Or maybe just fly
Expressing yourself will keep you alive

Before I sign out
I've just gotta say
These are the ones
With whose texts I have prayed
For body and soul
An inner massage
When I've been beat down
Or out on a roll
Bob Dylan
Bob Marley
John Lennon
Bob rule
Old Skool
Skinnyman 'n' Yellowman
Even Lily Allen man
Dizzy Rascal
Pass the parcel
Pik 'n' mix
You choose who's next
Why not Oli Goather?
Some folks will say you can't
But you just gotta go there

Richard Allen

Give and Get

Time is slipping
Drip
Drip
Dripping
My life is sliding by
And all my dreams or so it seems
Ain't being realised

So now each day I sit and pray
I'm working on my plan
To get success through happiness
On my feet I'll land

Sands of time don't fall in line
Effortless not trying
I'm out of the loop
I'm cock-a-hoop
Feeling just fine

Give and get
Not just joy but bliss
Give and get
Not just life but your kiss
Give and get

Shadow

The shadow of a bird
Between my eye and the sun
Carrying my sadness
Carrying my wrongs

Twenty wing-beats wide
Twenty wing-beats long

Shadow of my peace
Between my heart and the sun
Carrying my hopes
Carrying my song

Richard Allen

Untitled photograph by the author

Breaking

Last week I was riding high
Sitting on my biggest lie
But now my dreams have passed through the
hour glass
I am too scared to claim a love that lasts

How many times must I build a life?
Have it all
But somehow just not quite
Bleed real blood and cry real tears
Yet live behind a glass wall of fear

With water in my veins
And the desert in my eyes
Like a caretaker sweeping up the sands of time
I am locking up after life has fled
My mourning will start
My soul is dead

A bird hanging the instant the wind stops
A yacht frozen on a wave-top
I cling to this moment
Shut my eyes and hope to be saved
It seems hope's all I have
So I must be brave

Richard Allen

The Sun and Moon

Do you really want a drunken song to sing and
sway and fall?
I'm not really a real rude boy
I'm not cocksure at all
I've tried to be a rebel
Wore a leather
Flipped the bird
But couldn't hide I was a real good boy
I was just a little turd

I'm not real proud of where I'm from although
I'm also not ashamed
I can no longer be really hurt when you call me
stupid names
I don't think it really matters if you enter stage
left or right
What I think's important is that inside you've
got some fight

To hell with all your history
To hell with all their rules
To hell with all the sadists who try to put you
down
They're the villains
They're the pricks
They're the clowns
And they're the fools
Just stand real firm on your own two feet
You're the one who makes the rules

Hold the sun and moon
Hold them in your heart
Stop the world from turning
The dream's within your grasp

Richard Allen

You Know It in Your Heart

Your mate said how it is
Your poetry and songs are where the truth is
That's where the love and romance looms
And you're a lover and a romantic aren't you?

But you wouldn't be the first or last to fall into
its blinding grasp
The promise that it will love you
Easier said than done so the saying goes
But if you sit still
And calm right down
Then you'll touch the place where you will
know

But how can you step out?
How do you find the space to lift your head and
look about?
Just like the wage slave who has no time to find
escape
You're trapped by the people who want a piece
of you
Trapped when you want to go out just to buy
some food

At least that's how it looks to me
I'm not even going to talk about what living a
false life can mean

But hey guess what?
It's just illusion
Just "So what"
Because shine or rain
You've still got your brain
Ahead of the game
Or behind
You own your own mind
And if you can still feel
You'll defeat the unreal

Richard Allen

INDEX OF POEMS

Lightning Source UK Ltd.
Milton Keynes UK

176778UK00001B/8/P